A MAGAZINE FOR FABRIC DIE CUTTING ENTHUSIASTS

Publisher/Editor-in-Chief
Ebony Love

Creative Director
Brian Boehm

Copy Editor
Anne DeRuiter

Technical Editor
Linda Smoker

Contributors
Katrina Chapman-Kahn, Amy Friend, Elaine Haselhuhn

Each issue of **Blocks to Die For!** contains several blocks with cutting & piecing instructions for the most popular fabric die-cutting systems. Are you missing a specific die? Our EDeN™ System translation charts show you all the options. Don't have a die cutter? Rotary cutting instructions are included too!

Block charts are always accompanied by a sample quilt layout, color key, and fabric requirements. Accelerate your learning with expert tips and tutorials, and find inspiration in the photos and sketches that appear in every issue.

Want more? Visit our website for additional content and information on purchasing kits for projects featured in each issue.

Library of Congress
ISSN 2168-1147 (print), ISSN 2163-9078 (online)
ISBN 978-1-938889-04-2 (print),
978-1-938889-05-9 (digital)
Copyright © 2011-2013 LoveBug Studios.
All rights reserved.

Additional print or digital issues may be obtained directly from:

Blocks to Die For!
c/o LoveBug Studios
100 S. Atkinson Rd. #116-388
Grayslake, IL 60030
http://blockstodiefor.com
editor@blockstodiefor.com

M000168017

Finalist in the 2013 Indie Book Awards!

Now in its 2nd printing

The BIG Little BOOK of
Fabric
Die Cutting TIPS

by Ebony Love

THE **BLOCKS**

TABLE OF CONTENTS

HODGEPODGE

29

THE **SCOOP**

CONTRIBUTORS

Katrina

CHAPMAN-KAHN is an award winning quilter and loves to teach quilting classes using a variety of techniques and patterns. Since acquiring her cutters, she has discovered a love for die cutting and enjoys sharing tutorials and projects for all types of quilters. See more of Katrina's work at **sunshowerquilts.blogspot.com.**

Amy

FRIEND is an art scholar, former curator, and die-cutting enthusiast. Amy uses sewing, quilting and pattern designing as a creative outlet when she needs a change of pace. Amy creates at **www.duringquiettime.com**

Elaine

HASELHUHN has dabbled in many crafts, but sewing remains one of her favorites. She started to sew in 2009 when she was expecting a baby. She started with a simple baby blanket, joined a few quilting bees and hasn't stopped since! Elaine blogs her sewing adventures at **dashasel. blogspot.com.**

It is autumn, and my thoughts keep turning to all the things for which I am thankful, which is appropriate with Thanksgiving so near. Your letters, phone calls, and comments about the magazine returning have really buoyed my spirits and let me know that we are doing the right thing.

It is autumn, and all I want to do is work on my quilts, even though the crisp fall air and turning leaves also beckon me to take long walks in knitwear and mittens. I feel this way in every season, so this isn't really news. I'm one of those year-round quilters who see every day as an opportunity to quilt, no matter what the weather might suggest otherwise or what inducements there may be to leave the house.

It is autumn, but as I flip though the pages of the magazine, it feels very much like a renewal of something familiar, as though spring were approaching instead of winter. Rather than dread the inevitable biting cold of the air coming off Lake Michigan, I'm celebrating this season like never before, because it includes the revival of something dearly loved and missed. The blocks featured in this issue have made an appearance in our pages previously, but the articles and features are all brand-new. I think it's a nice balance of old and new; familiar and unexplored.

It is autumn, and BtdF is back. Doesn't that make you glad?

I hope you enjoy the relaunch of the magazine; it's so much more than it was, and yet exactly what it should be. Instead of a team of one (with a little help from friends every now and again), we actually have a staff of writers, editors, and a real-life creative director. We're also now in digital and print, which is an exciting avenue to explore as we seek to get BtdF into more hearts and hands.

We're going to work our way up—slowly— to more frequent issues, and eventually subscriptions. For now though, just enjoy the colorful leaves on display within, where everything old is new again.

EDeN System

[E]QUIVALENT [D]IE [N]OTATION | SYSTEM

Blocks to Die For Magazine proudly uses the Equivalent Die Notation (EDeN) System™ for all of its block charts and patterns. EDeN began simply out of a need to make the magazine a little more user-friendly, but it has quickly grown into a much-needed resource and reference for die-cutting quilters everywhere. In case you are new to the magazine or need a refresher on EDeN, we include this overview in every issue.

What is the EDeN System?

The EDeN System stands for "Equivalent Die Notation System". It provides a simple way to bridge the gap between rotary cutting instructions and die-cutting systems by identifying dies with a common number (the EDeN Number) and cross-referencing them with the rotary equivalent. This is all contained in a chart to help you to determine which dies to use, identify equivalent dies across all major die-cutting systems, and easily translate patterns from rotary cutting to die cutting and vice versa. EDeN is about leveling the playing field for all quilters.

About the EDeN Chart

When you get a copy of the chart from the EDeN website (it's a free download), you'll see the EDeN Number on the far left of the chart, followed by the rotary cut size, and then each manufacturer's die listed by system. Simply locate the EDeN Number on the left column of the chart then follow it across to the column that has your die-cutting system and dies.

Let's look at an example from the chart so you can familiarize yourself with the notation.

EDeN™ Number	Cutting System			
	Rotary (cut size)	Sizzix®	AccuQuilt GO!®	AccuQuilt Studio™
SQ-3	Cut 3½" squares	656689—Sizzix Die-Strips, 3½" Wide **OR** 656683—Sizzix Die-Squares,	3" Finished (3½" Unfinished) 55032—GO! Strip Cutter 3½" **OR** 55006—GO! Square 3½"	50011, 50060— Studio Strip Cutter 3½" **OR** 50140, 50206— Studio Squares 3½"

EDeN Numbers have two parts, the **Shape Abbreviation** and the **Shape Size**.

The Shape Abbreviation tells you what shape to cut:

STR = Strip
SQ = Square

REC = Rectangle
HST = Half Square Triangle
QST = Quarter Square Triangle
SOP = Square On-Point
DIA = Diamond
CIR = Circle

Shape Size: This is expressed as a finished size, to make it easier to convert between cutting systems. In the example above, SQ-3 is a square that finishes at 3".

EDeN System

[E]QUIVALENT [D]IE [N]OTATION | SYSTEM

To express common fractions, you'll see numbers like this:

X = the finished size is exact— so SQ-3 indicates a square that finishes at 3".

X¼ = this adds ¼" to the finished size— so SQ-3¼ finishes at 3¼".

X½ = this adds ½" to the finished size— so SQ-3½ finishes at 3½".

X¾ = this adds ¾" to the finished size— so SQ-3¾ finishes at 3¾".

Special Notations for Strips and Rectangles

Strips assume they are cut on the length of fabric (LOF). This length should be specified in your pattern. In most cases, you'll cut the longest length that you can, cut your strips to the correct width, then piece the resulting strips to get the full length you need.

Rectangles will have two measurements for the width and length, e.g. REC-3 x 6, or REC-1½ x 6, and sizes stop at 12", which is the largest die that will allow rectangles to be cut. Rectangles longer than 12" are considered strips.

Using EDeN in a Pattern

Whenever a pattern includes EDeN instructions in this magazine, you will see the EDeN Numbers displayed for cutting sizes, rather than the rotary instructions you may be used to seeing. If a traditional pattern had instructions that looked like this:

• From blue fabric: cut four 3½" squares; cut three 6" squares, then cut in half along one diagonal; cut one 2" square.

Example Block Chart

Unit	8" finished	12" finished
A	SQ-2	SQ-3
B	HST-2	HST-3
C	REC-2x4	REC-3x6

The EDeN instructions would look like this:

• From blue fabric: cut four SQ-3; six HST-6; one SQ-1½.

You can see that the EDeN Notation is much more compact and doesn't take much space. It's great for those who plan to die cut as much as they can, but it can be a little awkward at first for those who are rotary cutting until you get used to the notation.

We recommend you label your dies with the EDeN Number on the edge so you'll know immediately whether you have the right dies to make the project.

Using EDeN in this Magazine

When you look at a Block Chart, you will see the units & block sizes listed as shown in the chart above.

You would use the Block Chart in conjunction with the EDeN Chart to determine which dies or rotary cut shapes you would need to successfully make the block.

Getting the EDeN Chart

The magazine includes an excerpt of the EDeN Chart containing only the dies used in this issue, but the complete EDeN Chart is posted online where everyone can access the latest version. Die manufacturers are constantly releasing new dies, so you should always get an updated chart directly on the EDeN website. (http://equivalentdienotation.com)

The website has more information on using the chart and links to resources where you can get more help if you need it. You will also learn more about shapes with special notations, and find other designers and publishers who use EDeN in their patterns.

COMING SOON

ADVENTURES IN Fabric Die Cutting

THE PYRAMID CUTTING CAPER

BY EBONY LOVE

JOIN DIANA CUTLER ON THE FIRST Die-Cutting Adventure!

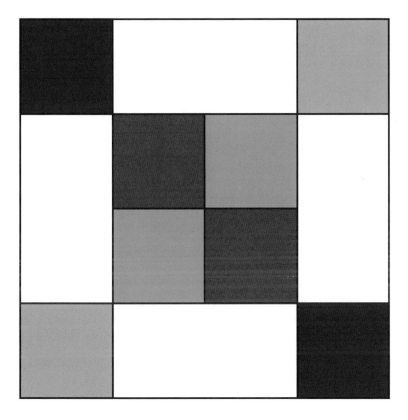

BLOCK CHART

Finished Block Size	Unit A	Unit B
6"	SQ-1½	REC-1½ x 3
8"	SQ-2	REC-2 x 4
10"	SQ-2½	REC-2½ x 5
12"	SQ-3	REC-3 x 6
16"	SQ-4	REC-4 x 8

CUTTING SYSTEM

Finished Block Size	BSP	GO!	Studio
6"	✔	✔	✔
8"	✔	✔	✔
10"	✔	✔	✔
12"	✔	✔	✔
16"	✔	✔	✔

Unit A Quantity/Color

2pc
2pc
2pc
2pc

Unit B Quantity/Color

4pc

BUILDING THE BLOCK

1

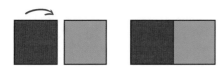

Sew 1 green Unit A to 1 red Unit A to make a two-patch unit. Press seams toward the red square. (Make 2)

2

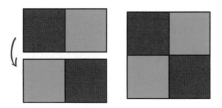

Sew the two-patch units together in a checker-board design to make the center square. Refer to the Tutorial: *How to Swirl a 4-Patch Seam* when pressing the seams.

Watch it here. **http://bit.ly/fourpatch**

3

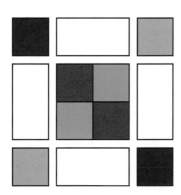

Lay out the center square, the 4 white B units, the 2 orange A units and the 2 blue A units in 3 rows of 3 units each as shown.

4

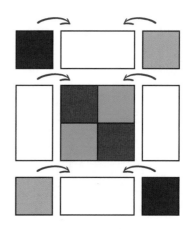

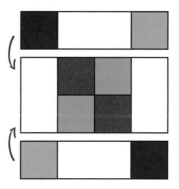

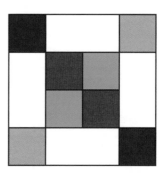

Sew the units together in each row. Press the seams in the top and bottom rows toward the center white B units. Press the seams in the center row toward the outer white B units. Join the rows. Press the seams toward the top and bottom rows to complete the Frayed Four Patch block.

BEYOND THE BLOCK—FRAYED FOUR PATCH

Don't be afraid to play with color in this block—it's a block that looks good in nearly every color combination, and you can alternate lights and darks to make different elements of the block stand out. It's also well suited for a scrappy quilt, and can go together quite quickly if you organize your scraps in advance, cut to size.

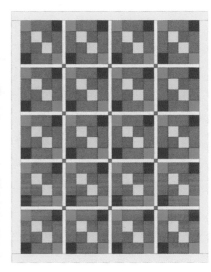

The Frayed Four Patch block is a fairly straightforward block to master, but what you may not recognize about this block is that you could make a bunch of these quickly by piecing strip sets and then sub-cutting the individual units.

For Unit A, cut strips in the specified size for the finished block (e.g. if you need an SQ-3, cut a STR-3 instead). For Unit B, cut a strip to the widest measurement first (e.g. if you need a REC-3 x 6, cut a STR-6).

Add some interest to your block units by using a narrow, contrasting sashing between the blocks, playing with different colorways, or setting your blocks in an unusual pattern.

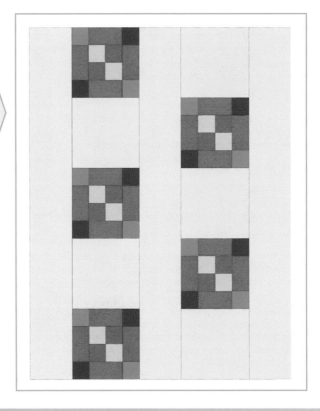

Marjorie Busby made an excellent video demonstrating this technique. This is why we **love** our strip dies!

Watch it here. **http://bit.ly/diecutfourpatch**

Most quilting companies reveal their new products twice a year at Spring and Fall Quilt Market. Market is typically held in mid-May and late-October each year; if you want to buy the latest dies, watch for those product reveals during that time!

The Equivalent Die Notation System (EDeN) is coming soon to a popular quilting magazine (besides this one). Keep your eyes peeled for the big announcement later this year!

Sizzix released a new version of the Big Shot. If you're strictly a quilter, the only noticeable difference is the aqua color and the fancy paint, but it's still a great machine for the price.

STUDIO OWNERS: if you're looking for new dies for your machine, you might want to consider turning to Sizzix and AccuCut for your next die fix. Both companies make dies that are compatible with the Studio (with the right adapters).

Did you know Ebony is now a frequent faculty member of the Original Sewing and Quilting Expo shows?

Check **sewingexpo.com** for a city near you to see her list of die-cutting classes!

Are you a fan of the Missouri Star Quilt Company? They just partnered with Sizzix to release 5 new dies based on some of their acrylic templates. However, if you're trying to make their Periwinkle Quilt using the Wacky Web template, you'll run into an issue achieving the point. MSQC wrote a blog post to explain how to correct your seam allowance for this quilt.

blog.missouriquiltco.com/how-get-the-periwinkle-point/

How many dies do you own? Take our poll and leave a comment! We'll reveal the most popular answers in the next issue.

polldaddy.com/poll/7200813/

Mark Your Calendars

World Quilt Show—Florida V in West Palm Beach, FL. January 9-11, 2014. **www.quiltfest.com**

Road to California Quilt Show in Ontario, CA. January 23-26, 2014. **www.road2ca.com**

AQS Quilt Week in Phoenix, AZ. February 5-8, 2014. **aqsshows.com**

Original Sewing and Quilting Expo in Lakeland, FL. March 20-22, 2014. **sewingexpo.com**

Original Sewing and Quilting Expo in Schaumburg, IL. March 27-29, 2014. **sewingexpo.com**

People ask me, "What's your favorite die?"

I'll always answer, "The 2½" strip cutter." It's so versatile, and it's the only die that never gets stored away because I use it almost every day.

—Ebony

GREEK SQUARE

BLOCK CHART

Finished Block Size	Unit A	Unit B	Unit C
6"	HST-2	SQ-2	REC-1 x 2
9"	HST-3	SQ-3	REC-1½ x 3
12"	HST-4	SQ-4	REC-2 x 4
15"	HST-5	SQ-5	REC-2½ x 5
18"	HST-6	SQ-6	REC-3 x 6
24"	HST-8	SQ-8	REC-4 x 8

CUTTING SYSTEM

Finished Block Size	BSP	GO!	Studio
6"	✔	✔	✔
9"	✔	✔	✔
12"	✔	✔	✔
15"	✔	Rotary cut Unit A	✔
18"	Rotary cut Unit A	Rotary cut Unit A	✔
24"	Rotary cut Unit A	✔	✔

A	B	A
A	B	A
B B	C	B B
A	B	A
A	B	A

Unit A Quantity/Color

4pc
4pc

Unit B Quantity/Color

4pc
4pc

Unit C Quantity/Color

1pc

BUILDING THE BLOCK

1

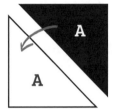

Sew 1 black Unit A to 1 white Unit A to make a corner square. Press seams open. (Make 4)

2

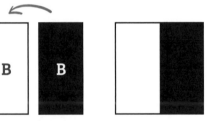

Sew 1 black Unit B to 1 white Unit B to make a side square. Press seams to the black. (Make 4)

2

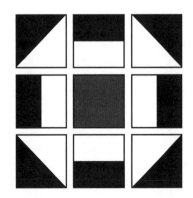

Lay out the 4 corner squares, the 4 side squares and the red Unit C square in three rows of three squares each as shown, noting the orientation of each square.

4

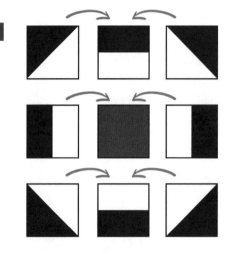

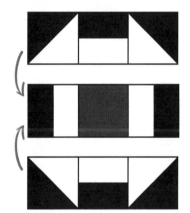

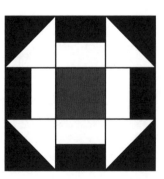

Sew the squares together in each row. Press the seams in the top and bottom rows toward the center square. Press the seams in the center row toward the outer squares. Join the rows. Press the seams toward the top and bottom rows to complete the Greek Square block.

BEYOND THE BLOCK—GREEK SQUARE

What is it about this color combination that draws us to use it again and again? There's just something about black, white, grey and red that makes any quilt look instantly sophisticated. This quilt has a wonderful graphic quality to it, and even though the block design is simple and quite traditional, the versatility of this block has timeless appeal.

If you're willing to experiment with the block coloring a bit and set this block on point, you can create a dramatic effect in a different way—the block is familiar, yet still fresh.

What are your favorite color combinations?

Strip Cutters Are Your Best Investment

I am frequently asked why anyone would purchase a strip cutter when they already own a rotary cutter and ruler. Even though the strip dies may seem like an extravagance at first, they really are the best value of all the die sets, no matter which cutting system you use. That is why, when I am asked which dies are the best to get when people first start die cutting, I always say, "The strip dies!" They are the absolute best work-horse dies because they do so much more than just cut strips.

Which Strip Dies?

If you can only buy one strip die, I would get the 2½" strip die. It's the most popular size for binding strips and there are many patterns on the market that work with the popular jelly roll strips of this size. Many quilters really enjoy making their own jelly rolls, and with the 2½" strip die you can quickly and easily cut them.

If you want to add other strip dies to your collection, consider the 1½", the 4½" and the 3½" strip dies, as these sizes work well with most standard block sizes. With just a few strip dies you can cut not only strips - but also squares, rectangles, parallelograms, diamonds and triangles. That's a lot of different shapes from just one die!

Marking Dies for Strips

To get all of these different shapes from the dies, we need to mark the dies with a permanent marker (silver is a good choice). First, mark the die blade lines down the length of your die—they are a little shorter than die board itself. Next, use a ruler across the die to help you mark the top and bottom edges of the die blades. Marking the place where the blades end will prevent you from laying fabric past the edge, causing an incomplete cut.

Marking for Squares and Other Shapes

Depending on the size strip on the die, mark additional horizontal lines to help you align your fabric for squares (photo 1). For example if you are marking the 2½" strip die, mark a horizontal line every 2½" along the die board. Also, mark the 45° line and the 60° line for parallelograms and diamonds. You can do this by aligning the 45° line and the 60° line on your ruler with one of the outer blades. You can do this marking on all of your strip dies, and they'll be ready when you are for your next project.

Watch this: **http://bit.ly/markstripdies**

photo 1

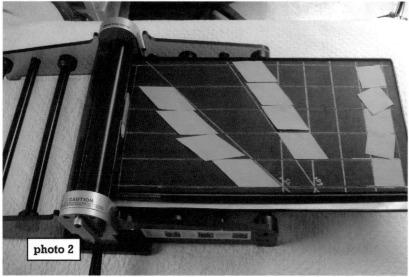

photo 2

8-pointed star, and the 60° diamond forms a 6-pointed one.

Cutting Shapes with Multiple Strip Dies

By adding in another size of strip cutter you can do even more! (photo 3) You can easily cut rectangles and parallelograms using two sizes of strips. If you lay your 2½" strips of fabric across the 4½" strip die, you can cut 2½" x 4½" rectangles. You can also center the diamonds you cut on the 2½" strip die across a die blade and get perfect isosceles triangles from the 45° diamonds and perfect equilateral triangles from the 60° diamonds. Feel free to mix and match the different strip dies to achieve different sized shapes.

Cutting Shapes with One Strip Die

All subsequent shapes start with a basic first strip cut, followed by sub-cutting. For example, if you want to cut squares, you would first cut strips, then rotate the fabric 90° and cut again for squares—using the lines you drew to help you align the fabric.

To cut diamonds, line up the edge of your strips with the 45° or 60° line to yield two different sizes of diamonds for blocks like Hunter's Star and Tumbling Blocks (see photo 2). The 45° diamond will form an

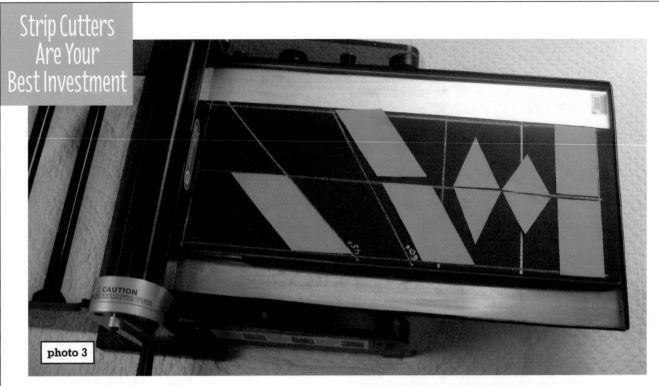

photo 3

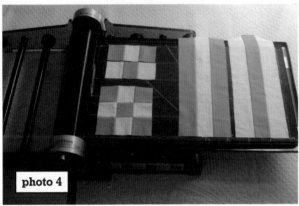

photo 4

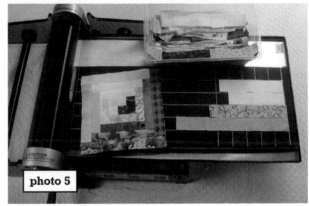

photo 5

Sub-cutting Pieced Units

The strip cutters can also be used to sub-cut strips of fabric that have already been sewn together for blocks like 4-patches and 9-patches (photo 4). First, cut strips using your strip die, sew the strips together into sets, and press the strip sets. Next, use the lines you drew on your strip cutter to line up the fabric strip sets across the die to sub-cut the strip sets into units. Sew these units together, and you have easy 4- or 9-patch blocks.

When using this technique, note that your seam allowances count as 1-2 additional layers (depending on whether you press open or to the side) so you need to consider them when you are layering your fabric for your particular cutter.

Bonus: Scrap-Busting!

The strip dies are also absolutely amazing for scrap busting (photo 5). The 1½" strip cutter is great for processing small scraps into useful bins of strips ready for log cabin blocks or pineapple blocks or any of the many variations of these blocks. Simply lay scraps across the die board until the desired layers are achieved and then run them through your cutter. In just a few minutes you will have useful strips cut perfectly and ready to be used in a quilt block.

Even though the strip dies seem expensive, they're the most economical dies you can purchase since they do so much more than just cut strips. Hopefully you see the strip dies differently now and can start using them to cut all these fantastic shapes!

MONKEY WRENCH

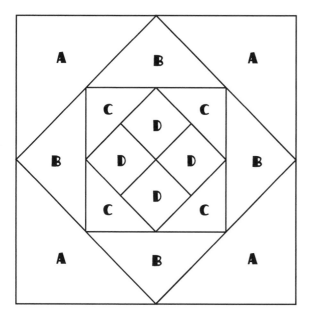

BLOCK CHART

Finished Block Size	Unit A	Unit B	Unit C	Unit D
6"	HST-3	HST-1½	QST-3	SQ-1
10"	HST-5	HST-2½	QST-5	SQ-1¾
12"	HST-6	HST-3	QST-6	SOP-3
16"	HST-8	HST-4	QST-8	SOP-4

CUTTING SYSTEM

Finished Block Size	BSP	GO!	Studio
6"	Rotary cut Unit C	✔	✔
10"	Rotary cut Unit D	Rotary cut Unit A, B, & C	✔
12"	Rotary cut Unit D	✔	✔
16"	Rotary cut Unit A & D	✔	✔

Unit A Quantity/Color

2pc
2pc

Unit B Quantity/Color

2pc
2pc

Unit C Quantity/Color

2pc
2pc

Unit D Quantity/Color

2pc
2pc

BUILDING THE BLOCK

1

Sew 1 purple Unit D to 1 yellow Unit D to make a two-patch unit. Press seams toward the purple square. (Make 2)

2

Sew the two-patch units together in a checkerboard design to make the center square.
Refer to the Tutorial: *How to Swirl a 4-Patch Seam* when pressing the seams.

Watch it here. **http://bit.ly/fourpatch**

3

Sew 2 purple Unit C's to opposite sides of the center square as shown, noting the orientation of the center square. Press seams toward the purple triangles.

4

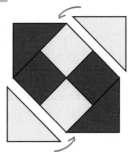 

Sew 2 yellow Unit C's to the remaining sides of the center square as shown to complete round one. Press seams toward the yellow triangles.

5

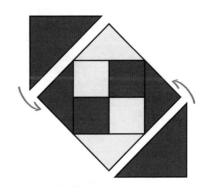

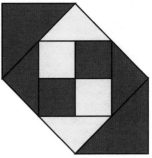

In the same manner, sew 2 purple Unit B's to opposite sides of the square as shown, noting the orientation of the square. Press seams toward the purple triangles.

BUILDING THE BLOCK (CONTINUED)

6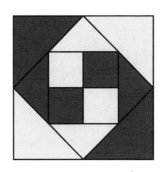

Sew 2 yellow Unit B's to the remaining sides of the square as shown to complete round two. Press seams toward the yellow triangles.

7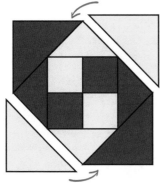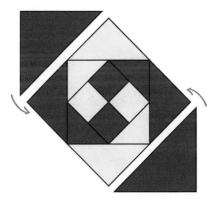

In the same manner, sew 2 purple Unit A's to opposite sides of the square as shown, noting the orientation of the square. Press seams toward the purple triangles.

8

Sew 2 yellow Unit A's to the remaining sides of the square as shown to complete the Monkey Wrench block. Press seams toward the yellow triangles.

BEYOND THE BLOCK—MONKEY WRENCH

This block is made up of a square, within a square, inside of a square within a square! The way it spirals around creates a great optical illusion, which is usually best preserved with a limited color palette.

If you orient all the blocks in the same direction, each block remains its own spiral, and you can see more clearly where a block begins and ends.

If you rotate every other block 90-degrees, you will get larger spirals that lock together and form an endlessly repeating pattern.

Even with a limited color palette, you can still make a fun quilt with the Monkey Wrench block. Consider working up this version as a child's play mat!

SUSANNAH BLOCK

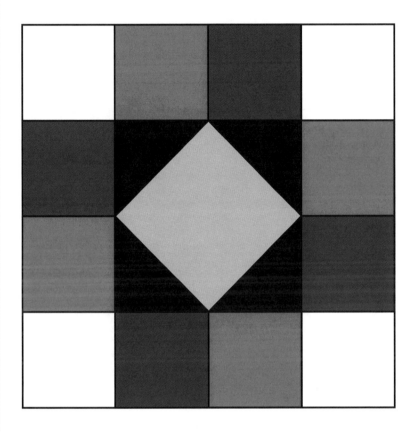

BLOCK CHART

Finished Block Size	Unit A	Unit B	Unit C
6"	SQ-1½	HST-1½	SOP-3
8"	SQ-2	HST-2	SOP-4
10"	SQ-2½	HST-2½	SOP-5
12"	SQ-3	HST-3	SOP-6

CUTTING SYSTEM

Finished Block Size	BSP	GO!	Studio
6"	Rotary cut Unit C	✔	✔
8"	Rotary cut Unit C	✔	✔
10"	Rotary cut Unit C	Rotary cut Unit B	✔
12"	Rotary cut Unit C	✔	✔

Unit A Quantity/Color
4pc
4pc
4pc

Unit B Quantity/Color
4pc

Unit C Quantity/Color
1pc

BUILDING THE BLOCK

 1

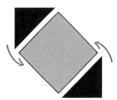

Sew 2 black Unit B's to opposite sides of the Unit C square. Press seams toward the black triangles.

 2

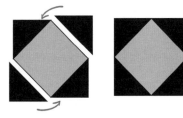

Sew 2 black Unit B's to the remaining sides of the Unit C square to make a center square. Press seams toward the black triangles.

 3

Sew 1 purple Unit A to 1 pink Unit A to make a two-patch unit. Press seams open. (Make 4)

 4

Sew a two-patch unit to opposite sides of the center square, noting the orientation of the two-patch units. Press seams toward the two-patch unit.

4

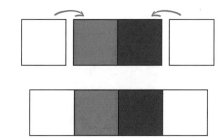

Sew a two-patch unit between 2 white Unit A squares to make a top/bottom row. Press seams toward to center two-patch unit. (Make 2)

6

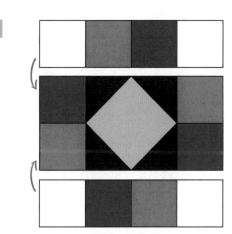

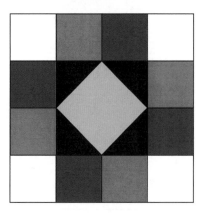

Stitch a top/bottom row to the top and bottom of the center square unit as shown, noting the orientation of the two-patch units. Press the seams toward the top and bottom rows to complete the Susannah block.

Beyond the block — Susannah Block

Oh Susannah! She's our featured pattern this month, and what we love most about the quilt being featured is the fabulous use of color. It is a perfect example of why it's great to have a collection of pre-cut fabrics in your scrap bin, just ready for a block like this to make them shine. Your strip dies are your friend here!

Still, if you want to use the color palette that makes Susannah the block she is, we recommend a contrasting sashing to set your blocks apart. The sashing can create secondary patterns and draw your eye to different elements depending on what you emphasize.

BY ELAINE HASELHUHN

Susannah's Play Date

(42" Wide Fabric)	12" Finished Block 51" x 51"
Blocks	Fat eighth each of 4-5 assorted prints in each color: red, orange, yellow, green, blue, purple, brown, gray and black
Background	1⅞ yards
Backing	3⅜ yards
Binding	⅝ yard
Batting	59" x 59"

CUTTING CHART – 12" FINISHED BLOCK

Unit	Color	Size	Subcut	Quantity	Used In...
A	Print #1	SQ-3	n/a	36	Blocks
	Print #2			36	Blocks
	Print #3			36	Blocks
B	Print #4	HST-3	n/a	36	Blocks
C	Print #5	SOP-6	n/a	9	Blocks
D		SQ-12	n/a	4	Background Squares
E		(2) 18¼ squares	Cut diagonally twice	8	Setting Triangles
F		(2) 9⅜ squares	Cut diagonally once	4	Corner Triangles
Binding		STR-2	n/a	6 WOF strips	Binding

1

A#3	A#2	A#1	A#3
A#1	B#4	B#4	A#2
A#2	C#5		A#1
A#3	B#4	B#4	A#3
A#3	A#1	A#2	A#3

Refer to the Susannah Block instructions; using the red prints #1, #2, and #3 A units, the red print #4 B units and the red print #5 C unit make a red Susannah block. In the same manner, make an orange, yellow, green, blue, purple, brown, gray and black Susannah block.

2

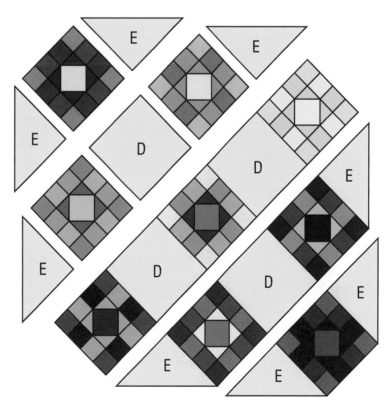

Lay out the nine blocks, the four 12½" D squares and the eight setting E triangles in 5 diagonal rows as shown. Sew the units together in each row. Press the seams in each row away from the blocks. Sew the rows together. Press the seams open.

3

Stitch a corner F triangle to each of the 4 corners to complete the quilt top.

4

Layer the backing (right side down), batting and quilt top (right side up). Quilt as desired. Trim the batting and backing even with the quilt top. Bind using your favorite method.

Elaine chose a bright orange thread and a square loop quilting design to finish the quilt. It's a simple, yet effective quilting pattern that can be done easily on a regular sewing machine using a walking foot. Try it on your next quilt!

Die Cuts Used for FREEZER PAPER STENCILING

Have you ever considered using die cut shapes to stencil your own fabric?
I love the challenge of using dies in unexpected ways; it's so nice when a single die can serve multiple purposes. It makes you really feel like you are getting your money's worth from it!

Lately, I have been exploring ways to use dies to create hand-printed fabrics that I can then incorporate into my sewing projects. It's actually a very simple process and uses easily obtained supplies: fabric, freezer paper, fabric paint, stencil brushes, and of course a die cutter and dies.

You will need to start with your base cloth which can be any kind of natural fiber material such as quilting cotton or linen. It's always best to prewash your material prior to printing—it ensures a better ink bond and also prevents later shrinkage. If you choose to work with print fabric instead of solid colors, you can stencil over it, but you need to make sure you have enough contrast between the print and your ink color so your design shows.

The stencil itself is cut with freezer paper which can be purchased in the grocery store in the same section as the aluminum foil and plastic wrap. For the paint, any textile paint or ink will work. You can buy fabric paint or fabric silkscreen inks in most craft stores or art supply stores. A stencil brush—with short, stiff bristles—is used to apply the ink.

The best dies for freezer paper stenciling are those that are fairly detailed, so you'll want to look at non-quilting dies for this process. Simpler dies with large

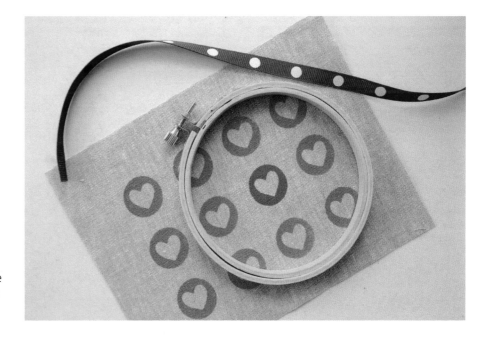

designs leave vast areas of ink and make for much stiffer fabric with little drape. Thinlits® by Sizzix are particularly good for freezer paper stenciling because they have such fine details. For these examples, I chose dies from the following sets:

► 658958—Sizzix Thinlits Die Set 6PK—Retro Camera & Icons (the heart within a circle)
► 658952—Sizzix Thinlits Die Set 6PK—Arrow, Banners, Chevron and Clouds (the chevron)

► 658944—Sizzix Thinlits Die Set 6PK—Butterflies and Flower Vine (the vine).

Though Thinlits are only intended to cut through one layer of paper, I was able to cut through 4 layers of freezer paper using the Thinlit and my die cutter since the freezer paper is so thin.

Once you have your shapes cut, lay them out on your fabric in a pleasing arrangement with the wax side facing

FREEZER PAPER STENCILING

down. You will be able to identify the wax side because it is shiny.

Here, the heart die cuts are arranged in a simple grid. The heart within the circle cut out was discarded and instead, the bit of freezer paper with the circle cut out was saved. Then, the loose heart was placed within. Any fabric not covered by freezer paper will be covered with ink. **(photo 2)**

Once all your pieces of die cut freezer paper are in place, carefully press with a warm iron. This will melt the wax on the bottom of the freezer paper and secure it to your fabric. Make sure that there is a good bond without any bubbles, especially along the edges where you will be applying the ink. You may want to mask the area around your stencil with additional strips of freezer paper so that stray ink doesn't end up on your fabric by accident.

Before you start painting, slide a piece of cardboard or a couple of layers of newsprint under your fabric so that the ink doesn't seep through to your work

surface. This is particularly important if you are using this technique to embellish clothing, such as a t-shirt, because you wouldn't want the ink to seep to the back side of the clothing.

Using your dry stencil brush with just a small amount of ink, tap the ink with an up and down motion into the cut out areas. Don't brush the paint on as you would when painting, because the ink is likely to seep under the edge of the stencil and you will not get a crisp image. Have fun playing with your design! **(photo 3)**

Your ink will need a number of hours to dry thoroughly before revealing your design. I like to stencil in the evening and then go to bed, removing the temptation of removing the paper too early. By the morning, it is dry.

Once the ink is completely dry, peel off the freezer paper to reveal your hand printed fabric design! You will need to follow the manufacturer's directions

photo 3

photo 2

to set the ink. They often involve heat setting with your iron. Sometimes you just need to wait a period of 72 hours for the ink to cure prior to washing. It is sometimes possible to use your freezer paper stencil a second time if you are able to remove it without ripping it.

You can also layer different stencils on your project to combine designs. You just follow the same process, by stenciling one image **(see photo 4)** allowing it to dry, and following the process to remove the stencil and set the ink. Then layer your next stencil (making sure you also mask the area of the first stencil you painted) and repeat the process. That's

how I added the blue flowers to this vine. **(photo 5)**

Freezer paper stenciling can be used in so many ways. It can be used to embellish clothing as suggested above. Pieces of stenciled fabric can be fussy cut as the focal point of a pouch or bag or used as-is. They can be treated as you would any piece of fabric and incorpo-

rated into patchwork. Think about running your stenciled fabric back through the die cutter using a quilting die or other shape. You could even stretch your hand-printed fabric in a hoop and hang it. **(photo 6)**

I hope that you find this tutorial inspiring and are ready to create some amazing stenciled fabric!

Editor's Note: The dies referenced in this article can be used in the Sizzix Big Shot and Big Shot Pro, as well as the AccuQuilt Studio with the appropriate adapters. To use this technique in any of the AccuQuilt GO! machines, you will need to use GO! dies.

photo 4

photo 5

photo 6

EDeN™ System Chart

EDeN™ Number (finished size)	Rotary (cut size)	Sizzix®	AccuQuilt GO!®	AccuQuilt Studio™
STR-1	Cut a LOF strip X 1-1/2" wide	656680—Sizzix Bigz XL 25" Die—Strips, 1 1/2" Wide use the lengthwise grain for borders	55024, 55075—GO! Strip Cutter 1 1/2" OR 55164—GO! Strip Cutter—1", 1 1/2", 2" (use 1 1/2" strip) use the lengthwise grain for borders	55052, 50065—Studio Strip Cutter 1 1/2" use the lengthwise grain for borders
STR-1½	Cut a LOF strip X 2" wide	657633, 656687—Sizzix Die—Strips, 2" Wide use the lengthwise grain for borders	55025, 55073—GO! Strip Cutter 2" OR 55164—GO! Strip Cutter—1", 1 1/2", 2" (use 2" strip) use the lengthwise grain for borders	55054, 50611—Studio Strip Cutter—2" use the lengthwise grain for borders
STR-1¾	Cut a LOF strip X 2-1/4" wide	NONE	55053—GO! Strip Cutter—2 1/4" use the lengthwise grain for borders	50055—Studio Strip Cutter—2 1/4" use the lengthwise grain for borders
STR-2	Cut a LOF strip X 2-1/2" wide	656681, 656688, 658328, 658330—Sizzix Die—Strips, 2 1/2" Wide use the lengthwise grain for borders	55014, 55017—GO! Strip Cutter 2 1/2" use the lengthwise grain for borders	50056, 50612—Studio Strip Cutter 2 1/2" use the lengthwise grain for borders
STR-2½	Cut a LOF strip X 3" wide	657634—Sizzix Bigz XL 25" Die—Strip, 3" Wide use the lengthwise grain for borders	55084—GO! Strip Cutter—3" use the lengthwise grain for borders	50010, 50058—Studio Strip Cutter—3" use the lengthwise grain for borders
STR-3	Cut a LOF strip X 3-1/2" wide	656689, 657898—Sizzix Die—Strips, 3 1/2" Wide use the lengthwise grain for borders	55032, 55074—GO! Strip Cutter—3 1/2" use the lengthwise grain for borders	50011, 50060—Studio Strip Cutter—3 1/2" use the lengthwise grain for borders
STR-3½	Cut a LOF strip X 4" wide	NONE	55085—GO! Strip Cutter—4" use the lengthwise grain for borders	50012, 50061—Studio Strip Cutter—4" use the lengthwise grain for borders
STR-4	Cut a LOF strip X 4-1/2" wide	657643—Sizzix Bigz Pro 25" Die—Strips, 4 1/2" Wide use the lengthwise grain for borders	55054—GO! Strip Cutter 4–1/2" use the lengthwise grain for borders	50013, 50062—Studio Strip Cutter 4 1/2" use the lengthwise grain for borders
STR-5	Cut a LOF strip X 5-1/2" wide	NONE	55026—GO! Strip Cutter—5 1/2" use the lengthwise grain for borders	50607—Studio Strip Cutter—5 1/2" use the lengthwise grain for borders
STR-6	Cut a LOF strip X 6-1/2" wide	658685—Sizzix Bigz Pro 25" Die—Strip, 6 1/2" Wide	55086—GO! Strip Cutter—6 1/2" use the lengthwise grain for borders	50047, 50609—Studio Strip Cutter—6 1/2" use the lengthwise grain for borders

EDeN™ System Chart

EDeN™ Number (finished size)	Rotary (cut size)	Sizzix®	AccuQuilt GO!®	AccuQuilt Studio™
SQ-1	Cut a strip 1-1/2" wide; subcut to 1-1/2"	STR-1	STR-1	50199, 50601–Studio Square–1 1/2" **OR** STR-1
SQ-1½	Cut a strip 2" wide; subcut to 2"	STR-1½	55022–GO! Square–2" **OR** STR-1½	50201, 50602, 50709–Studio Square–2" **OR** 50748–Studio Square–2", 3", 4", 5" (use 2" shape) **OR** STR-1½
SQ-1¾	Cut a strip 2-1/4" wide; subcut to 2-1/4"	NONE	STR-1¾	STR-1¾
SQ-2	Cut a strip 2-1/2" wide; subcut to 2-1/2"	656674, 656682, 657607–Sizzix Die–Squares, 2" Finished **OR** STR-2	55059–GO! Square 2 1/2" Multiples **OR** 55018, 55021 – Value Die (2 1/2" Square) **OR** STR-2	50124, 50204, 50603–Studio Square–2 1/2" **OR** STR-2
SQ-2½	Cut a strip 3" wide; subcut to 3"	657606–Sizzix Bigz Die–Square, 2 1/2" Finished **OR** STR-2½	STR-2½	50016, 50132, 50749–Studio Square–3" **OR** 50748–Studio Square–2", 3", 4", 5" (use 3" shape) **OR** STR-2½
SQ-3	Cut a strip 3-1/2" wide; subcut to 3-1/2"	656683, 657608–Sizzix Die–Squares, 3" Finished **OR** STR-3	55006–GO! Square 3 1/2" **OR** STR-3	50140, 50206–Studio Square–3 1/2" **OR** STR-3
SQ-4	Cut a strip 4-1/2" wide; subcut to 4-1/2"	657609–Sizzix Bigz Die–Square, 4" Finished **OR** STR-4	55018, 55021–Value Die (4 1/2" Square) **OR** 55060–GO! Square–4 1/2" Multiples **OR** STR-4	50015, 50123 – Studio Square–4 1/2" **OR** STR-4

EDeN™ System Chart

EDeN™ Number (finished size)	Rotary (cut size)	Sizzix®	AccuQuilt GO!®	AccuQuilt Studio™
SQ-5	Cut a strip 5-1/2" wide; subcut to 5-1/2"	657635–Sizzix Bigz Pro Die—Square, 5" Finished	STR-5	50131, 50207–Studio Squares—5 1/2" OR STR-5
SQ-6	Cut a strip 6-1/2" wide; subcut to 6-1/2"	657264–Sizzix Die—Square, 6" Finished OR STR-6	55000 – GO! Square 6 1/2" OR STR-6	50070, 50286–Studio Squares—6 1/2" OR STR-6
SQ-8	Cut a strip 8-1/2" wide; subcut to 8-1/2"	657265–Sizzix Die—Square, 8" Finished	55058–GO! Square—8 1/2"	50211–Studio Square—8 1/2"
SQ-12	Cut a strip 12-1/2" wide; subcut to 12-1/2"	NONE	NONE	50021–Studio Square—12 1/2"
REC-1 x 2	Cut a strip 2-1/2" wide; subcut to 1-1/2"	STR-2 AND STR-1	STR-2 AND STR-1	STR-2 AND STR-1
REC-1½ x 3	Cut a strip 3-1/2" wide; subcut to 2"	STR-3 AND STR-1½	55158–GO! Rectangle—2" x 3 1/2" OR STR-3 AND STR-1½	50808–Studio Rectangle—2" x 3 1/2" OR STR-3 AND STR-1½
REC-2 x 4	Cut a strip 4-1/2" wide; subcut to 2-1/2"	657605–Sizzix Die—Rectangle, 2" x 4" Finished OR STR-4 AND STR-2	55159—GO! Rectangle—2 1/2" x 4 1/2" OR STR-4 AND STR-2	50130–Studio Rectangle—2 1/2" x 4 1/2" OR STR-4 AND STR-2
REC-2½ x 5	Cut a strip 5-1/2" wide; subcut to 3"	657624–Sizzix Die—Rectangle, 2 1/2" x 5" Finished OR Rotary cut a strip 5-1/2" wide AND STR-2½	STR-5 AND STR-2½	50138–Studio Rectangle—5 1/2" x 3" OR STR-5 AND STR-2½
REC-3 x 6	Cut a strip 6-1/2" wide; subcut to 3-1/2"	657625–Sizzix Die—Rectangle, 3" x 6" Finished OR STR-6 AND STR-3	55005–GO! Rectangle 3 1/2" x 6 1/2" OR STR-6 AND STR-3	50037, 50146–Studio Rectangle—3 1/2" x 6 1/2" OR STR-6 AND STR-3

EDeN™ System Chart

EDeN™ Number (finished size)	Rotary (cut size)	Sizzix®	AccuQuilt GO!®	AccuQuilt Studio™
REC-4 x 8	Cut a strip 8-1/2" wide; subcut to 4-1/2"	658113—Sizzix Bigz XL Die—Rectangle, 4" x 8" Finished OR Rotary cut a strip 8-1/2" wide AND STR-4	55160—GO! Rectangle-4 1/2" x 8 1/2" OR Rotary cut a strip 8-1/2" wide AND STR-4	Rotary cut a strip 8-1/2" wide AND STR-4
HST-1½	Cut a 2-3/8" square; cut in half along one diagonal	656676—Sizzix Bigz L Die—Half-Square Triangles, 2" Finished Square	55319—GO! Triangles 1 1/2" Finished OR 55048—GO! Bountiful Baskets (2" cut)	50771—Studio Half Square—1 1/2" Finished Triangle
HST-2	Cut a 2-7/8" square; cut in half along one diagonal	656685, 657611—Sizzix Die—Half–Square Triangles, 2 1/2" Finished Square	55018, 55021—Value Die (2 1/2" Triangles) OR 55063—GO! Half Square—2" Finished Triangle Multiples	50161, 50272—Studio Half Square—2" Finished Triangle
HST-2½	Cut a 3-3/8" square; cut in half along one diagonal	657610—Sizzix Die—Half-Square Triangles, 3" Finished Square	NONE	50162, 50275—Studio Half Square—2 1/2" Finished Triangle
HST-3	Cut a 3-7/8" square; cut in half along one diagonal	656686, 657612—Sizzix Die–Half-Square Triangles, 3 1/2" Finished Square	55009—GO! Half Square— 3" Finished Triangle OR 55048—GO! Bountiful Baskets (3 1/2" cut)	50163, 50278—Studio Half Square—3" Finished Triangle
HST-4	Cut a 4-7/8" square; cut in half along one diagonal	657613, 657677—Sizzix Die—Half-Square Triangles, 4 1/2" Finished Square	55031—GO! Half Square—4" Finished Triangle	50000—Studio Square—4 7/8" (cut in half on the diagonal) OR 50005, 50270—Studio Half Square—4" Finished Triangle
HST-5	Cut a 5-7/8" square; cut in half along one diagonal	657637—Sizzix Die—Half-Square Triangles, 5 1/2" Finished Square	NONE	50273—Studio Half Square—5" Finished Triangle

EDeN™ System Chart

EDeN™ Number (finished size)	Rotary (cut size)	Sizzix®	AccuQuilt GO!®	AccuQuilt Studio™
HST-6	Cut a 6-7/8" square; cut in half along one diagonal	657638– Sizzix Die–Half-Square Triangles, 6 1/2" Finished Square	55001–GO! Triangle 6 1/2"	50033, 50276–Studio Half Square–6" Finished Triangle
HST-8	Cut a 8-7/8" square; cut in half along one diagonal	NONE	55400–GO! Half Square 8" Finished Triangle	50798–Studio Half Square–8" Finished Triangle
QST-3	Cut a 4-1/4" square; cut in half along both diagonals	NONE	55396–GO! Quarter Square 3" Finished Triangle	50792–Studio Quarter Square–3" Finished Triangle
QST-5	Cut a 6-1/4" square; cut in half along both diagonals	657620–Sizzix Bigz L Die–Triangle, 3 1/8"H x 5 1/2"W Unfinished	NONE	50274–Studio Quarter Square–5" Finished Triangle
QST-6	Cut a 7-1/4" square; cut in half along both diagonals	657621–Sizzix Clear Die–Triangle, 3 5/8"H x 6 1/2"W Unfinished OR 657171–Sizzix Die–Triangles, 3 1/2"H x 6 1/2"W Unfinished	55002–GO! Triangle 4 7/8"	50034, 50277–Studio Quarter Square–6" Finished Triangle
QST-8	Cut a 9-1/4" square; cut in half along both diagonals	657639–Sizzix Bigz XL Die–Triangle, 4 5/8"H x 8 1/2"W Unfinished OR 657172–Sizzix Die–Triangles, 4 1/2"H x 8 1/2"W Unfinished	55399–GO! Quarter Square 8" Finished Triangle	50790–Studio Quarter Square–8" Finished Triangle
SOP-3	Cut a strip 2-5/8" wide; subcut to 2-5/8"	NONE	55394–GO! Square on Point– 2 1/8" Finished	50799–Studio Square on Point–2 1/8" Finished (2 5/8" Cut)
SOP-4	Cut a strip 3-5/16" wide; subcut to 3-5/16"	NONE	55317–GO! Square–3 1/4" (use a scant 1/4" seam)	50128–Studio Square on Point–3 1/4"

EDeN™ System Chart

EDeN™ Number (finished size)	Rotary (cut size)	Sizzix®	AccuQuilt GO!®	AccuQuilt Studio™
SOP-5	Cut a strip 4" wide; subcut to 4"	NONE	STR-3½	50014, 50136, 50750, 50751—Studio Squares—4" OR 50748—Studio Square—2", 3", 4", 5" (use 4" shape) OR STR-3½
SOP-6	Cut a strip 4-3/4" wide; subcut to 4-3/4"	NONE	55019—GO! Square—4 3/4"	50035, 50144—Studio Square on Point—4 3/4"

© Ebony Love, 2011-2013. You may freely copy these charts for personal use. Full versions available on http://equivalentdienotation.com

A Few Notes

- All block sizes are stated in finished block measurements, assuming a ¼" seam allowance unless otherwise indicated.

- Blocks will be charted in as many sizes as possible using dies for all units, up to 24", as space permits.

- Sometimes, it is necessary to substitute a die shape that is a bit larger than needed in order to make a block which finishes at the specified size.

  These dies will be included if the unit can be easily squared-up to the correct size after piecing. These will be noted in the block charts.

- When a strip cutter is specified by itself for a unit that is square, you are meant to use the strip cutter to cut strips, then rotate the strips 90° on the same die and re-cut the fabric to make squares.

- When a strip cutter is specified to cut diamonds, you are meant to cut strips first, then rotate the strip the indicated number of degrees to cut diamonds. This will be easier if you mark your dies in advance.

- When a strip cutter is shown in combination with another die (e.g., 2" strip cutter AND 3½" strip cutter), this is an indication to cut strips on one die, then rotate 90° and layer on the second die to cut rectangles.

- Fabric yardage is assumed to be 42" wide and rounded up to the nearest ¼ yard, and is calculated ONLY for the original block given. Please note that the quilt layouts provided have not been personally tested; you are encouraged to perform your own fabric calculations if you need to be more accurate.

- **WOF** = width of fabric; **LOF** = length of fabric; **RSU** = right side up; **WSU** = wrong side up; **RST** = right sides together.

empty wallet

We certainly like to shop and spend money, but it's a lot more fun spending other people's money. Here is an opportunity or two to relieve yourself of some cash in utterly evil ways...

Mystery Quilt Along

Sponsored by
ANDOVER FABRICS

DO YOU LOVE DOWNTON ABBEY?

Do you love to die cut fabric? Then join the **Mystery Quilt Along** for a thrilling mixture of suspense, cutting tips, new blocks to try, and luscious fabric from Andover Fabrics.

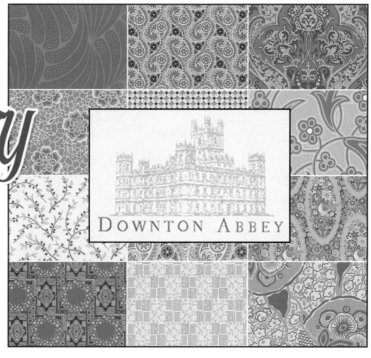

NOVEMBER 10 / 2013
lovebugstudios.com

A limited selection of fabrics and Downton-themed items are available for purchase, and you can choose your favorite character—**the Dowager Countess**, **Lady Edith**, **Lady Mary**, or **Lady Sybil**.

Mystery Quilt Kit— BACKING SET $78.75	Set of Six 1" Shank Buttons $10.50	Fabric by the Yard $10.50

Check availability and purchase information at
lovebugstudios.etsy.com

For more Quilt Along details, visit **lovebugstudios.com/downtonabbey**

Made in the USA
Charleston, SC
27 December 2013